MICROSOFT OUTLOOK QUICK START 2024 GUIDE

JEXONIA GRANEER

INTRODUCTION

Welcome to the "Microsoft Outlook Quick Start 2024 Guide," a comprehensive resource designed to help both new and experienced users navigate the ever-evolving landscape of Microsoft Outlook. This guide is tailored specifically to the 2024 version of Outlook, which, like its predecessors, continues to redefine efficiency and productivity in professional and personal communication.

The Evolution of Microsoft Outlook

Microsoft Outlook has long been a cornerstone in the world of digital communication, evolving from a simple email client to a robust platform for managing a wide range of communication and scheduling tasks. The 2024 version of Outlook builds upon this rich history, introducing new features and integrations that promise to enhance user experience and streamline daily workflows.

Why Choose Outlook 2024?

Outlook 2024 is more than just an email application; it's a comprehensive tool designed to facilitate communication and organization in a highly connected world. It's equipped to manage multiple email accounts, schedule meetings, set reminders, and seamlessly integrate with a plethora of other applications. This guide aims to unlock these capabilities for you, whether you're just starting out or seeking to deepen your existing knowledge of Outlook.

A Guide for Everyone

The "Microsoft Outlook Quick Start 2024 Guide" is structured to cater to a diverse audience. Whether you're a novice looking to understand the basics or a seasoned user aiming to exploit Outlook's advanced features, this guide has something for everyone. It is meticulously designed to ensure that each reader can navigate through Outlook's interface, understand its core functionalities, and utilize its advanced features for maximum productivity.

Building a Solid Foundation

For those new to Outlook or upgrading from a previous version, understanding the interface and basic functionalities is crucial. This guide begins by laying a solid foundation, ensuring that you're well-prepared to utilize Outlook to its full potential. You'll learn about setting up your account, customizing your workspace, and navigating through Outlook's primary features.

Exploring the Depths of Outlook

Microsoft Outlook is renowned for its multifaceted capabilities. This guide delves into the depths of these features, demonstrating how Outlook goes beyond mere email management. You'll discover how to effectively organize your emails, manage your calendar, handle your contacts, and keep track of your tasks, all within a single interface.

Streamlining Your Workflow

One of the key advantages of Outlook 2024 is its ability to integrate with other applications and services, significantly enhancing its functionality. This guide explores these integrations and teaches you how to leverage them to streamline your workflow and increase your productivity.

Mastering Email Communication

At its core, Outlook is about managing email communication effectively. This guide provides detailed insights into creating, sending, and organizing emails. It covers everything from basic email etiquette to advanced techniques for managing large volumes of emails, helping you to become an email communication expert.

Enhancing Productivity with Shortcuts

Efficiency in Outlook can be significantly boosted through the use of keyboard shortcuts. This guide includes a comprehensive list of shortcuts specific to Outlook 2024, tailored to save you time and enhance your productivity.

Embracing Modern Communication

In the digital era, where communication speed and efficiency are vital, Outlook 2024 stands as a beacon of modern communication. It has been refined to handle the complexities and demands of today's interconnected world. This guide will show you how to navigate through its interface with ease, ensuring that you can keep up with the rapid pace of digital communication.

Customization: Making Outlook Your Own

One of the most powerful aspects of Outlook 2024 is its ability to be customized to fit your personal and professional needs. This guide explores the myriad of customization options available, from simple aesthetic changes to complex rule creation for email management. You'll learn how to tailor Outlook to work for you, turning it into a personal assistant that aligns with your unique workflow.

Beyond Email: A Hub of Productivity

Outlook 2024 transcends its identity as an email client. It's a hub for your daily activities, integrating email management with calendar events, task lists, and contact management. This guide will explore how these features interact seamlessly, providing you with a holistic view of your daily, weekly, and monthly schedules. You'll discover how to synchronize your tasks and appointments, making sure you're always on top of your commitments.

Advanced Features for the Power User

For the power users, Outlook 2024 offers a plethora of advanced features and functionalities. This guide will cover these in detail, including how to use Outlook's powerful search capabilities, manage large volumes of emails, and utilize advanced calendar functions. You'll learn to leverage these features to manage your time and tasks more effectively, turning Outlook into a powerhouse of productivity.

Security and Privacy in the Digital Age

In an age where digital security and privacy are of utmost importance, Outlook 2024 offers robust features to protect your information. This guide will provide insights into the security and privacy settings of Outlook, ensuring that your communications remain secure and your personal information stays private. You'll learn about encryption, spam filters, and other security measures that are essential in today's digital landscape.

Collaboration and Teamwork

Outlook 2024 is not just about individual productivity; it's also a tool for collaboration. This guide will show you how to use Outlook for team collaboration, including sharing calendars, organizing meetings, and managing group tasks. You'll discover how Outlook can be a central tool in facilitating teamwork and communication within your organization or personal projects.

Navigating the Changing Landscape of Digital Communication

As we progress through this guide, you'll notice that Outlook 2024 is a reflection of the changing landscape of digital communication. This guide will not only teach you how to use Outlook effectively but also provide insights into the trends and practices in digital communication. You'll learn to adapt to these changes, using Outlook as a tool to stay ahead in a world where staying connected is crucial.

Conclusion

As we embark on this journey through the "Microsoft Outlook Quick Start 2024 Guide," remember that this book is more than just a manual. It's a pathway to mastering a tool that's vital in today's digital age. By the end of this guide, you will not only have a thorough understanding of Outlook 2024 but also the skills to use it as a powerful tool for communication and organization.

By the end of this guide, you will not only be proficient in using all the features that Outlook 2024 has to offer, but you will also have a deeper understanding of how digital communication tools can enhance your productivity and connectivity. Whether you are managing your personal life or professional engagements, the skills and knowledge you gain from this guide will empower you to use Outlook 2024 as a tool to achieve more, in less time, with greater efficiency.

Welcome to the "Microsoft Outlook Quick Start 2024 Guide." Let's embark on this journey to master Microsoft Outlook 2024 and transform the way you communicate and organize in the digital age.

CONTENTS

CHAPTER 1: GETTING STARTED WITH MICROSOFT OUTLOOK

What is Microsoft Outlook?

In today's digital era, where communication has become lightning-fast and extremely efficient, tools that facilitate this rapid exchange of information have become indispensable. Among these tools, Microsoft Outlook stands out as one of the most prominent and widely used platforms. But what exactly is Microsoft Outlook?

Definition and Core Purpose

Microsoft Outlook is a personal information manager software system from Microsoft. While it's primarily used as an email application, it also includes a variety of other tools such as a calendar, task manager, contact manager, note-taking, journal, and web browsing. Outlook is a part of the Microsoft Office suite, though it can be purchased separately and used on its own.

The Email Functionality

Email remains at the core of Outlook's functions. It provides users with an integrated platform to send, receive, and organize their emails. With robust filtering options, users can categorize emails, flag important messages, and even divert unwanted emails into a junk folder. This ensures that primary emails stand out, reducing the chance of missing essential communication.

Integrated Calendar and Scheduling

One of Outlook's standout features is its calendar functionality. Users can schedule meetings, set reminders, and mark important dates. The integrated nature of Outlook means that an email can be quickly converted into a calendar event. For instance, if you receive an email about a meeting, with just a few clicks, you can set a reminder in your calendar without manually entering all the details.

Task Management and Organization

Beyond email and calendar, Outlook provides a comprehensive task management system. Tasks, ranging from simple to-do items to complex projects with multiple steps, can be organized, prioritized, and tracked. As tasks are completed, they can be marked off, and if they're tied to specific dates or meetings, they can be integrated with the calendar feature.

Contacts at Your Fingertips

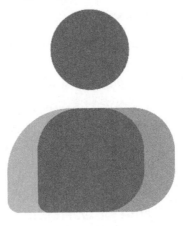

Outlook's contact manager is another feather in its cap. Users can store detailed information about their contacts, including email addresses, phone numbers, physical addresses, birthdays, and even anniversaries. This information can be synched across devices, ensuring you have the details you need wherever you go. It's also integrated with the email function, allowing for quick and easy communication.

A Unified Dashboard

What truly sets Outlook apart from many other email platforms is its unified dashboard. Instead of toggling between different applications or web pages for email, calendar, tasks, and contacts, everything is available in a singular view in Outlook. This consolidation increases efficiency and reduces the time spent searching for specific information or functionalities.

Outlook Across Devices

While initially designed as a desktop application, the evolution of technology and the rise of mobile devices have seen Outlook expand its reach. Today, there are dedicated Outlook apps for smartphones and tablets, ensuring that users remain connected and have access to their data on the go. These apps maintain the core functionalities of the desktop version but are optimized for mobile use.

Safety and Security

SAFETY & SECURITY

In an age where data breaches and cyber threats are rampant, Outlook takes security seriously. With advanced filters, it keeps malicious emails at bay. Furthermore, data encryption ensures that personal and sensitive information remains safe. Microsoft continuously updates its security protocols to counter emerging threats, giving users peace of mind.

Integration with Other Microsoft Products

Outlook's potency is further amplified when used in tandem with other Microsoft Office products, like Word, Excel, and PowerPoint. For instance, an Excel sheet can be quickly attached to an email, or a PowerPoint presentation can be shared with contacts seamlessly. This integration makes it an essential tool for professionals and casual users alike.

In Conclusion

Microsoft Outlook is not just an email client. It's a comprehensive personal information manager that streamlines various functionalities into a unified platform. From sending emails to scheduling meetings, from managing tasks to keeping track of contacts, Outlook serves as a one-stop solution for personal and professional communication needs. Its widespread use globally is a testament to its efficiency, reliability, and robustness. Whether you're a student, a professional, or someone looking to organize their digital life better, Outlook offers tools that are both powerful and user-friendly.

A Brief History of Outlook

The tale of Microsoft Outlook begins in the mid-1990s, a period of rapid technological advancement and the dawning era of widespread digital communication. When we trace back the lineage of this renowned personal information manager, we uncover a fascinating journey of innovation and evolution.

Microsoft Outlook was introduced to the world in 1997 as part of the Microsoft Office 97 suite. It was developed as a successor to Schedule+, a previous Microsoft program, and was initially branded as "Outlook 97". The initial version laid the groundwork, offering email services integrated with a calendar, task manager, and contact database. Even in its infancy, Outlook showcased the potential to revolutionize workplace communication.

As the digital era progressed, so did Outlook. By the early 2000s, Microsoft released several updates to accommodate the evolving needs of users and to ensure compatibility with newer operating systems. Outlook 2003, for instance, offered improved email and spam filtering, reflecting the growing concerns over cyber security and the increasing volume of digital correspondence.

One of the significant leaps for Outlook was its integration with Microsoft Exchange Server. This merger allowed for collaborative features like shared calendars and mailboxes, rendering Outlook indispensable in professional settings, especially large corporations.

As technology became increasingly mobile, Outlook adapted. Recognizing the shift from desktops to laptops and then to smartphones and tablets, Microsoft developed versions of Outlook tailored to these devices. The introduction of Outlook Mobile in 2015 was a significant milestone, ensuring that users could access their data and stay connected, irrespective of their device or location.

In its essence, the history of Microsoft Outlook is a testament to adaptability and foresight. From its humble beginnings as a desktop email client to its current status as a multifaceted communication tool available across platforms, Outlook's journey mirrors the broader trajectory of digital communication over the past few decades. Through its continuous updates and refinements, Outlook remains as relevant today as it was when first introduced, standing tall as a beacon in the realm of personal information management software.

Outlook's Role in Modern Communication

In the intricate tapestry of modern communication, Microsoft Outlook stands as a pivotal thread, weaving together various modes of digital interaction. As our means of communication have diversified and grown in complexity, Outlook has steadfastly evolved, ensuring its relevance and indispensability in contemporary scenarios.

First and foremost, Outlook transcends the role of a mere email client. While emails remain an integral method of professional correspondence, the demands of the modern world necessitate a more holistic approach. Outlook responds by offering a unified platform where users can not only send and receive emails but also schedule meetings, set reminders, manage tasks, and maintain a comprehensive contact list. This multi-functionality ensures that communication is seamless and consolidated, reducing fragmentation and potential oversights.

Another significant facet of Outlook's contribution to modern communication is its adaptability to remote working environments. The recent shift towards telecommuting and digital workspaces has emphasized the need for tools that facilitate collaboration across distances. Through its integration with Microsoft Exchange Server and Microsoft Teams, Outlook supports shared calendars, synchronized inboxes, and collaborative task management. Such features enable teams, irrespective of their physical locations, to function with a sense of unity and coherence.

Additionally, the modern communication landscape is characterized by a blend of professional and personal interactions. Outlook acknowledges this by providing features that cater to both realms. While its integration with other Microsoft Office applications (like Word and Excel) bolsters its professional utility, its user-friendly interface, customizable settings, and mobile applications make it apt for personal use as well.

In conclusion, Outlook's role in modern communication is multifaceted and profound. It serves as a bridge, connecting various elements of digital interaction into a cohesive whole. By consistently adapting to the changing dynamics and needs of users, Outlook not only retains its significance but also reinforces its position as a cornerstone in the edifice of modern communication tools.

The Evolution of Features Over the Years

Since its inception, Microsoft Outlook has been a beacon of innovation and adaptability in the realm of personal information management software. Its journey, spanning over two decades, reflects a commitment to user-centricity, always evolving to meet the changing demands of the digital age.

The initial release of Outlook in 1997 was a watershed moment, bringing together email, calendar, task manager, and contact management in one platform. Even then, it was evident that Microsoft aimed for an integrated communication tool rather than just an email client.

Over the next few years, as cyber threats became more pronounced, Outlook 2003 introduced improved spam filters, reflecting the product's adaptability to the digital challenges of the times. This edition also enhanced its visual appeal, bringing in the iconic Navigation Pane and introducing the Reading Pane for emails, which allowed users to preview messages without fully opening them.

With the release of Outlook 2007, there was a noticeable push towards better integration with other Microsoft Office applications. The Ribbon, a feature that provided quick access to commands, was introduced. This version also boasted superior search capabilities, making email and data retrieval more efficient.

Outlook 2010 took integration a step further with the introduction of the "People Pane," which offered quick insights into contacts and their interactions. Social connectors were added, allowing users to get real-time updates from their social networks right within Outlook.

Mobile communication's explosion couldn't be ignored, and Outlook responded with dedicated mobile apps, ensuring connectivity on the go. Features like Focused Inbox, introduced in later versions, sorted emails based on relevance, helping users prioritize their correspondence.

One of the most recent evolutions has been the seamless integration with cloud services. Users can now easily save attachments directly to OneDrive, facilitating better data management and sharing.

In essence, the trajectory of Outlook's features over the years paints a picture of a product in constant metamorphosis, always staying ahead of the curve, and redefining the standards of digital communication tools.

Outlook vs. Other Email Clients: A Comparison

When it comes to email clients, the market offers a plethora of options. Microsoft Outlook, over the years, has carved its niche, but how does it stack up against its competitors?

Functionality & Integration: While most email clients offer standard features like sending and receiving emails, Outlook distinguishes itself with its integrated calendar, task manager, and contact database. Its seamless synchronization with other Microsoft Office applications makes it a holistic communication tool.

User Interface: Clients like Thunderbird or Apple Mail have intuitive interfaces, but Outlook's unified dashboard, which brings emails, calendar events, and tasks into one view, often proves to be a game-changer for many users.

Customization & Extensions: Gmail, with its browser-based interface, offers numerous extensions via the Chrome Web Store. While Outlook might seem restrictive in comparison, its extensive settings and integrations, especially in the business environment with add-ins, provide robust customization.

Security: In terms of security, Outlook, with its advanced spam filters and enterprise-grade security protocols, often has an edge, especially when integrated with Microsoft Exchange.

In summary, while individual preferences play a role, Outlook's comprehensive features, integration capabilities, and security measures often make it a top choice, especially in professional settings.

Overview of the 2023 Upgrade

The Microsoft Outlook 2023 upgrade is a testament to the software's enduring commitment to innovation and user-centric development. This latest iteration brings forward a suite of enhancements that align with the evolving needs of the modern digital communicator.

Enhanced User Interface: 2023 introduces a cleaner, more intuitive design, making navigation effortless. The refined UI also supports better customization, allowing users to personalize their workspace further.

Advanced AI Integration: Leveraging the power of AI, the new Outlook offers smarter email categorization, predictive text, and improved search functionalities. These features not only boost productivity but also ensure a smoother user experience.

Collaborative Features: Building on the remote work trend, the 2023 upgrade bolsters collaborative tools. Real-time co-authoring and seamless integration with Microsoft Teams make group projects and communication more efficient.

Security Upgrades: In an era where cyber threats are rampant, Outlook 2023 fortifies its security protocols, providing users with advanced phishing protection and improved spam filters.

In essence, the 2023 upgrade reaffirms Outlook's position as a forward-thinking, comprehensive communication tool, primed for the challenges of the modern digital age.

Setting Expectations: What You'll Learn in This Guide

Welcome to the Microsoft Outlook 2024 Edition Guide for Beginners! As you delve into these pages, you're embarking on a journey to master one of the most powerful communication tools available today. Here's a brief overview of what to expect:

- **Foundational Knowledge:** We'll start with the basics, giving you a firm grasp of what Outlook is, its historical progression, and its pivotal role in today's digital communication landscape.
- **Navigational Skills:** Learn to effortlessly move within Outlook's interface, ensuring that you can access its multitude of features with ease and confidence.
- **Functional Mastery:** From managing contacts to setting up meetings and organizing tasks, we'll provide step-by-step guidance, ensuring you utilize Outlook to its fullest potential.
- **Comparison Insights:** Gain an understanding of how Outlook stands in comparison to other email clients, helping you appreciate its unique strengths.

- **Update Highlights:** Stay abreast of the latest features introduced in the 2023 upgrade, ensuring you're leveraging the newest tools and functionalities.

By the end of this guide, you'll be well-equipped to harness the power of Outlook 2023, optimizing both your professional and personal digital communication.

CHAPTER 2: UNRAVELING OUTLOOK'S CAPABILITIES

A Glimpse into the Latest Features of Outlook

Outlook is dedicated software for personal management; it also helps you to manage your Email effectively. So, in this section, we would be finding out the real standout features of Outlook mail. And they are;

Efficient Email Management; This is an outstanding feature that shouldn't be ignored. You can manage your work email and categorize them based on your needs, thereby avoiding any form of confusion and giving you the ease of operation you need. Besides that, you can also execute flagged commands to receive emails quickly.

Ability to sync data on/off your devices; This feature helps you to be able to work and manage mail with more flexibility. All you need is a phone or device connected to the network and then login into your Microsoft account; you can collect all related information and work with them more easily.

Retrieving Forgotten Passwords

To reset your password, you'll have to know your old password; this is done to secure all related information. Proceed by login into the application, and on the settings page, you go to the security section. You will see an option right there to change the password.

If you've forgotten your old password, click 'I forgot my password' and follow the instructions to reset your password.

Not able to find the download files on your device

You can view all of this by clicking Documents in the Oracle Content application navigation menu and proceed by clicking Offline in the filter menu. When you're done downloading the file, it is downloaded to a secure area within the Oracle Content Application. You're able to access it through the mobile application, even if you aren't connected to the cloud.

But for security reasons, it is impossible to be accessed outside the Oracle Content so that you won't find it in your regular download folder or any other folder on your device.

Please Note: If you're using an IOS device and have saved the file locally to your device, you can view it in the file application.

To delete a synchronized or downloaded file, tap and hold the file, select it, and proceed by tapping the delete icon.

Removing these files from your device wouldn't affect the original copy, which has been stored in the cloud.

Locating Downloaded Files

To view such a file, all you need is the right software on your device. Now, for example, if you downloaded a PDF file, you'll need an app on your device that would be able to open the PDF file. If you don't have the correct app, you'll not be able to view the file.

Perk: One of the latest features introduced by Microsoft is the ability to enable dark mode. This is only available in office 365.

For the dark mode, all you have to do is sign in to Outlook. Click 'Try new Options,' and a new function will immediately be activated.

Accessing the Visible and Invisible in Outlook

Outlook reminds you to attach a file and never miss a flight again. Also, add the details to the flight automatically.

Outlook reminds you of a task you've never specified or an appointment you'd forgotten to write down.

If you compose an email and type the words, Outlook would remind you that you may have forgotten to attach the file. You can stop such a sending process, attach a file, and send a message. For more Outlook functions, you can click Attach files or Insert Pictures in Outlook email messages.

Well, have you also found yourself in an email conversation that you wish to ignore? Perhaps, you work in a large company, and someone could annoyingly add you to a distribution list without your consent. Instead of deleting each message from the conversation, you can ignore or delete the entire conversation.

All messages in the conversation would be moved to the Deleted Items Folder. Future messages from that conversation would be wholly skipped from your inbox and placed directly to the Deleted Items Folder.

You can use a clean folder to wipe out extra and unnecessary messages.

Suppose you've emailed a lot of workers when you only needed a few of them, well, here's what to do. First of all, the cause is that you used text effects like bold, underline or even bright font colors to make your names stand out.

Now here' what you should do, type @ followed by the name, and an operation will immediately happen.

The name would be automatically added to the recipient line of the email message. So, when the recipient does receive a letter in their inbox, they'll see the @ symbol in the message list.

Search folders; the actual case in this category could be that a user needs to regularly do specific searches. You can create a virtual folder that consists of the items that meet specific search criteria.

In this sense, Outlook does have a series of templates or custom folders that would be created. For example, we can find the unread items folder, which includes emails located in various folders. It's also important to know that no mail is physically transferred to the search folder but can be displayed in that location virtually by meeting the specified criteria.

Effortless Procedures for Beginners

Click on the folder tab, and choose 'New Search Folder.' In such a time, you can select an already created template or simply customize a search folder.

In such a case, find the last option in the list Custom, select it, and click Choose in the New Search Folder dialogue box.

Next, select a name for the search folder you are creating and click on Criteria, which specifies the search criteria.

Scheduling your Email; Perhaps you wish to set the time and date other than the time to write something down. It is possible to do it differently, also quite simple.

Here's the procedure; first of all, you proceed as if it were regular mailing, and that's whether it is a new one or a response to one received.

Next up, and from the message itself, you click the Options Tab and proceed to Delay Delivery in the More Options Sections.

Then you select the box, make sure you 'Do Not Deliver Before' and select date and time; this is when you want the message to be sent. Choose any other option you so desire and Click Close.

Outlook is known to store scheduled email messages in your Outbox until they are further needed when transferred to your Sent Folder. In any case, it's always possible to change the date or time of the deferred Delivery or cancel it.

To do this, proceed to Outbox; this is where you'll be able to find the Email, open it and click the Options and Deferred Delivery tab; in which you can make all the changes you do feel it's appropriate.

Open Multiple Windows; if you use Outlook for Email, tasks and scheduling, you may also want to open multiple Outlook windows. This permits you to view your Email, tasks and calendar consecutively. You don't have to use the navigation buttons to keep switching views. It also gives you the freedom to use the different trays at the same time too.

Smart Searches; With Outlook, you can search for your preferred content, both in specific mailboxes and in subfolders, folders and all generalized forms. But what isn't well known is this, we can also refine searches by applying particular strategies.

Writing a single word (Ontek), the engine will display all elements containing that word, without discriminating between the upper and lower case.

Now, if we write two words (Blog Ontek), the engine would show us those elements that contain one or two words or even both, regardless of the order.

If we use quotation marks (Blog Ontek), the elements that do contain the exact string will be displayed.

To customize a quick step, all you have to do is click on 'Create New' in the 'Quicksteps section.' Following this, a Quickstep would open, and you must name it. Then you proceed by choosing the action that we want to associate with it and click on the 'Add Action.'

What you are doing here is this, you are adding as many actions as we do need for this Quickstep; for example, we can configure quick steps to mark a message as necessary or as 'Unread' and transfer it to the 'Emails to reply' folder. In such a way, all actions that would require various steps to execute can be simplified with a single combination of keys.

If you'd receive a flight, hotel, or rental car reservations by Email; with this Outlook will automatically add them to the calendar along with the related information, such as the tracking number, confirmation, and link.

Unfortunately, Outlook cannot calculate travel time to the airport, so be sure to check out the traffic before you leave so that you don't arrive late.

Favorite Folders; 'Favorites' is a tab located at the top of the folder panel, and the function of this tab is simply to facilitate access to the most used folders. This is done to prevent you from scrolling or searching through numerous or panels of folders, which can be quite discouraging to start with.

All you have to do is drag those you need now as 'Favorites,' and they will be visible there, all as if they were direct access. By moving them within the favorites, we can have them to satisfy us the most.

Perhaps you wish to remove the folders from 'Favorites,' all you need to do is right-click on it and choose 'Remove from Favorites.' And, you'll have to know it is a 'Live' folder, which is especially suitable when operating different tasks at hand.

Why Users Love Outlook

One of the fascinating things about Outlook is the number of functions to operate your tasks efficiently. It spans from managing your contacts to creating and assigning tasks and printing attractive mailing labels to managing your digital schedule. Outlook can do all of it.

Outlook is also known to organize all of your emails, Calendars, contacts, tasks and to-do-lists in just one space. Its organization starts with your email account; from there, you can begin working on your Email, transitioning to work or appointments, and storing information about the people you interact with the most in your contacts. All these are done so that you don't have to remember email addresses or phone numbers. Let's take a quick look at some of the essential functions;

You can use Outlook to send and receive emails that'll be used to communicate with people inside your organization and outside.

It can also be used to schedule all-important appointments on your calendar and manage appointments to remind you before the meeting.

You can store additional contact details such as; your company name, telephone number, address, and other information.

Outlook also permits one to send high capacity files much more easily and quickly.

It has the best features to block spam emails, mark or block special emails more safely and effectively.

Permits the use of HTML and CSS; this is done to help you be more creative in sending mail. Perhaps, you accidentally delete your messages while using it; you can apply the 'Quick Recovery Feature.'

The Efficiency Edge of Outlook

It permits sign in with temporary passwords and able to star essential messages. Suppose you wish to use that password for a certain period; all you have to do is automatically set up the settings. The form would be attached to 'Important Messages' so that when they are sent, they'll be notified first, which is a more convenient way to make your exchange.

The function of sorting emails by time, size, ending time, and time of receiving. So you can find your Email and file you need to send.

Also known to support it with large file attachments combined with SkypeDrive or OneDrive.

You can block Email by specific address or domain (which is highly resistant to spam) Generates a disposable email address (used for one-time mailing operations or Email Marketing); this is done to keep you away from spam mail engines. With Outlook, you can create, change and delete these addresses more easily.

Supports recovered or deleted emails, which is all within the acceptable amount of time, even when deleting the trash's emails.

Access to unlimited storage.

Permits logging in with a temporary password. Integrates Skype for chatting through Skype.

Outlook is also known to save time; a quick step in Outlook is a small macro you do have to create. And you can use such a macro over and over again. You don't need any programming skills to make a quick step. Creating a Quickstep is much more comfortable.

All you have to do is click the necessary actions together, and all the activities together become one Quickstep. You have the liberty to forward a specific email, ad a piece of text and then place the Email in your archive. You can bring those three steps altogether in one Quickstep. Extra time is the result of making Quicksteps.

Scheduling emails: Perhaps you wish to create an email and want it to be sent early tomorrow morning. All you have to do is save the Email in your draft folder and send it before tomorrow. Another option is to indicate in the email options that your Email shouldn't be shipped till a certain point in the future. This is where it only has one drawback, nonetheless, at that specific moment, your Outlook should be working, and your computer mustn't be turned off; your Outlook must be overall active.

Using your daily task lists under your calendar, a daily task list is a handy tool that permits you to show tasks from your to-do-list at the bottom of your calendar. Under the calendar, you can put a subset of your more extensive list in your to-do-list.

Able to manage important mails for users to see first; All other mail parts are kept separately.

You can also quickly search mails by type.

There's a shortcut function for archiving, scheduling messages and deleting. You can switch between apps, Email and calendar all at a glance.

Able to send large files instantly without loading them to the device.

Developing several Outlook Templates; if you regularly have to write the same Email, all you have to do is use the option to create Outlook templates.

You create a template in the following way, make the 'template mail,' and that's done by creating a new mail.

Type your text, the subject line for the recipients (to, cc, bcc) save the Email via File> Save As...> Outlook template.

You can also save the template file in another template file in another folder. To apply the template, go to New Items> Choose Form and then go to your 'User Template in File System.' if you've saved the template in another folder, you can proceed to use the template by double-clicking the file. It's also possible to use the template in a rule. This allows you to have emails automatically answered, especially when an email lands straight in your inbox that meets all conditions.

Using an additional Calendar to write time, time tracking is one of the best ways to increase awareness of your actions. Having someone follow you all day can costs you some cash. All you have to do to resolve this is to create a different calendar. To do this, create a new folder and choose the calendar items as the folder's content.

When you are working, open your calendar or your timekeeping calendar; drag the actions from your daily task list to the time in your timesheet calendar; that's when they are completed.

If you don't do an action from your list, add it manually from your calendar. You'll get an overview of what you did on a particular day.

It is also helpful because it gives you feedback on what you did in the past week. An insight that helps you do better than next week.

Permits incoming grouping mail, filters private messages by individual's/business messages in the inbox.

Outlook also permits one to send high capacity files.

CHAPTER 3: MASTERING CONTACTS, CALENDARS, AND TASKS

Learn how to create and manage your Contacts list, including changing how you view your contacts, attaching photos to them, and sending them to other people, as well as how to sort your contacts and use grouped views.

Discover how to create and modify appointments, print your calendar, and work with multiple calendars using the Calendar.

In addition to allowing you to keep your entire list of names and addresses in one place, Outlook also lets you sort, view, find, and print it in many different ways, depending on the type of work you're doing. Furthermore, you can store lists of family and friends alongside your business contacts in Outlook, so you can easily distinguish between them when necessary.

Inputting Contacts: Basics to Advanced

Keeping a large number of names, numbers, and addresses is not difficult, but finding them again in the future requires magic unless you have an application like Outlook. Several programs can save names and related numbers, but Outlook is the most popular choice for working with names, addresses, and phone numbers.

You'll be familiar with the Outlook Contacts feature if you've ever used a pocket address book. You just need to enter the name, address, phone number, and a few tidbits-and you're done!

The quick and dirty way to enter contacts.

A new contact can be added easily to your Contacts list:

To create a new contact, click the New Contact button in the People module. A contact form will appear.

Complete the form. It is not necessary to fill out all the fields; only use those that pertain to the contact in question.

Close the document by clicking Save & Close. It's really that simple. Adding more information to contact later is okay if you don't fill in all the details immediately.

Detailed Contact Compilation

Depending on your preferences, you can enter literally dozens of details about every person on your contacts list. However, if you just want to include the essentials, that's fine. Here's what you'll need to do to enter every tiny detail for every contact record.

Select "New Contact" from the People module.

You will see the new contact form.

Choose your full name from the drop-down menu. A window titled "Check Full Name" appears.

Take one or more of the following actions:

To scroll down, click the triangle (called the "scroll-down button") on the right edge of the text box named "Title." You can either type a title (such as Reverend, Guru, or Swami) or select one from the drop-down menu.

Enter the contact's first name in the first text box.

If necessary, type the contact's middle initial (if any). Leave this field blank if there is no middle initial. The middle name can also be written here if you wish.

Enter the contact's last name in the "Last" text box.

Select the suffix from the drop-down menu. Select one of the options (like Jr., III, or Ph.D.), or type one in the box (such as D.D.S., B.P.O.E.).

To proceed, click the OK button.

Your Full Name and File NumberAs text boxes are now filled with the name you entered in the Check Full Name dialog box,

Complete the form by clicking on the appropriate box and entering the requested information.

Please leave the box blank if the information is unavailable, for example, if a contact does not have a title. There are more options when a triangle appears after the box. If your choice isn't listed, enter it in the box.

When you enter a name in the Full Name box, you'll see that name appear in the File As box.

You can file a person under a different name by clicking File As and entering the designation you prefer. Your dentist may, for example, be filed under the term "dentist" rather than by name. In the alphabetical listing, the dentist's name appears under "dentist" rather than under the actual name. In your contacts list, you will find the full name and the file as designations. By doing so, you can find your dentist either by name or by the word "dentist."

Enter the email address of your contact in the "Email" text box.

To enter a second email address, click Email 2, pick the second address from the list, and then enter it in the text box.

Type the business phone number of the contact in the text box beside "Business Phone."

You will have the option to type in the contact's home phone number if you click on the Home Phone text box.

In order to enter numbers other than home and business telephones, click the triangle beside the number option, choose the type of number you are entering, and then enter the number.

There are four blocks for phone numbers in the New Contact form. The drop- down menu contains 19 different types of phone numbers that you can use according to the types of numbers your contacts have.

Choose the type of address you want to enter in the Addresses section by clicking the triangle.

Choose either a business address, a home address, or some other address.

Go to the Addresses section and click the button. An address check dialog box appears.

Fill in the appropriate fields with the following information:

The street The city, state, The province

Region of zipping or postal code Country

Click OK to close the Check Address dialog box.

If the address you just entered will be used for mailing, select the "This Is the Mailing Address" box on the New Contact form.

If you want the address card to link directly to a page, click in the Web Page Address text box and type the page's address.

A contact's webpage can be viewed by opening a contact record, clicking on the More button on the Ribbon, and clicking Web Page (or pressing Ctrl+Shift+X).

An internet browser will display the webpage.

The URL of the page can be viewed in your web browser by entering it into the Address box. Within the Web Page Address text box, you can enter the URL for any webpage an Outlook contact has.

Fill in the bottom right notes box with whatever information you want.

There is no limit to what you can enter (preferably something that will help in your dealings with the contact).

Click the Save & Close button on the Ribbon after you are finished.

When you've entered any information you need (or may need) to know about the people you deal with at work, you're ready to start interacting.

Viewing the contacts

The information you enter in Outlook can be viewed in many different and useful ways, called views. By viewing your contact information and sorting the views, you can easily see the big picture of the data you've entered. Within each module, Outlook provides several predefined views. You can edit any predefined view, name it, save it, and then use it exactly as you would the predefined views.

You can change how your contacts list appears by following

these steps:

Select the Home tab from the Ribbon of the People module.

Choose the view you want from the Current View group. That view will appear on the display. Besides the card view, you can also select the phone view, the list view, or any other view you like.

View Sorting

A few views, such as the phone view of the People module, are organized as simple lists.

You can sort by a column's title once you've clicked on its title if you can't find a contact in a view with columns. Suppose you want to know the names of the IBM employees in your contacts list. If you sort the company column, you can see all the names at the same time.

Here are the steps you need to follow to sort by column name:

Select the Phone view on the Ribbon under the Current View section of the People module.

Contacts are displayed in the phone view.

Go to the COMPANY column and click the heading.

Contacts are listed alphabetically from A to Z (or ascending order) according to the "company" column. Now you can find someone by scrolling to that letter. By sorting by company, all contacts appear in alphabetical order of company name.

Upon clicking the title a second time, you will see your contacts sorted in reverse alphabetical order (i.e., descending order).

Rearranging Views

Simply drag the title of a column and drop it where you want it to appear to rearrange the appearance of a view. Below is an example of how to move

The contacts list may already be displayed in the phone view.

To the left of the FILE AS column, click on the title of the preferred column and drag it over.

Red arrows appear to the left of the clicked column, pointing to the border between two columns. By releasing the mouse button, Outlook will drop the column where the red arrows indicate.

Let go of the mouse button. You have now dragged the column from the right to the left. The procedure is the same for moving any column in Outlook.

Using grouped views

Sorting doesn't always suffice. After a while, you can easily accumulate several thousand contacts; it only takes a few years. In a long list, if you're looking for something with the letter M, for instance, you'll find it about three feet below the bottom of the screen, regardless of how you sort it.

There is no need for Outlook, Anonymous groups are the solution. You already have several predefined lists that rely on grouping in Outlook.

Lists are displayed in Outlook in several different ways: Sorted lists are like playing cards laid out in numerical order, starting with twos and proceeding to threes, fours, and so on, up to picture cards. In a group view, all the hearts, the spades, the diamonds, and then the clubs are arranged together in a single row.

Here are the steps to viewing the company grouping in list view: Select the Home tab under the People module.

Select the List option from the Current View group on the Home tab.

Companies are represented by headings with the prefix "company". The number of items under each heading is shown under that heading.

Expanding or collapsing the contacts under that heading is done by clicking the triangle symbol to the left of the heading.

You can group items according to just about anything you want, provided that the data you enter is accurate.

Below are the steps for grouping by another field:

Select View Settings from the View tab of the People module.

A dialog box with advanced view settings for the list appears. You will see that Group By is set to "company."

Group by clicking "group by."

An appropriate dialog box opens. You will see that Group Items By is set to "Company."

Select a different field from the company list.

Specify the sort order by clicking "Ascending" or "Declining."

Ascending means going from A to Z, and descending means going from Z to A. For the dialog box to close, click OK.

Close the Advanced View Settings: List window by clicking OK.

Identifying Your Friends

A string tied around your finger doesn't do much to remind you to do something that involves another person, and it looks ridiculous as well. Fortunately, Outlook provides a better solution. You can easily remember the name of someone you have promised to call next week by flagging their name in the Contacts list. This will trigger a reminder in your calendar. Flagging isn't limited to contacts. The same effect can be achieved by adding reminders to tasks, emails, and appointments.

The following steps will guide you through the process of adding flags to contacts:

You can flag a contact by right-clicking on it in the People module. You'll see a shortcut menu appear.

Select Follow Up. "

You will see the "Follow Up" menu. Choose the day for your follow-up.

You have the option of choosing today, tomorrow, this week, or next week. When you flag a contact for a specific day, that contact's name appears in your Outlook Calendar on that day.

Select the contact, click "Follow Up," then add a reminder. A dialog box appears.

If you need to avoid that person for some reason, you can choose to have the reminder open and a sound played at the time you specify. Reminders are Outlook's way of telling you to do something.

The Custom dialog box allows you to select a reminder date from the Date drop- down menu in the Reminder section.

A calendar is displayed when the arrow next to the date is clicked. Click on the date you want.

] From the drop-down menu, select a time for a reminder. Set the reminder by clicking OK.

Finding a contact from any Outlook module

You'd like to search for a person, but you're currently using another module. That's fine. Any Outlook module can be searched using the Search People box on the Home tab on the Ribbon. The steps are as follows:

Find people by clicking on the "Seek People" box.

You will find it on the far right of the Home tab of any Outlook module.

Enter the contact's name.

To open that contact's record in Outlook, press Enter.

When you enter only a few letters of a name, Outlook lists names that contain those letters, so you can choose the contact you had in mind. With the word "Wash," you can search for George Washington, Sam Washburn, and any other people on your list that include "Wash."

To view a contact record, double-click its name.

Sending a business card

Any Outlook user (or any other application that is capable of displaying digital business cards) is able to forward an electronic business card to another Outlook user. There's no better way to share any contact record in your list with someone else.

The most obvious thing you may want to send this way is your own contact information.

Create your own contact record in the People module.

This record should contain all the information you need to send to someone.

To send information to a contact record, click twice on the record. Clicking twice opens the contact record.

From the Ribbon, click the Forward button under the Contact tab.

Three options are provided: as a business card, as an internet card (vCard), or as a contact in Outlook.

Select the format that suits you best.

If you're unsure, select "Business Card." Both Outlook and Internet cards can be sent using that program. A new message is generated containing the contact information.

Enter the recipient's address in the "To" text box.

You can also choose a name from your address book by clicking the "To" button.

Press Alt+S (or click the Send button).

A message and vCard will be sent to the recipient.

Double-clicking the icon representing the business card in the message will add the business card to your Contacts list. An additional contact record will be created. You can now add the new name along with all the information on the business card to your contacts list by clicking the Save and Close button.

Alternatively, your business card can be forwarded by clicking the contact record and then selecting the Forward button in the Ribbon. The process is shorter, but you can only forward it as a business card or as an Outlook contact.

CHAPTER 4: INTEGRATING AND EXPANDING WITH OUTLOOK

In this chapter, we will delve more deeply into how Outlook works, its components, and how much can be achieved without spending a lot of time trying to figure out how things work. Carefully go through the points outlined below to gain more knowledge.

Outlook and Other Programs

Lots of users prefer to use Outlook as their email client and personal information manager. Over the years, Outlook, as part of the Microsoft Office Suite, has proven to be a standard solution (in conjunction with the Microsoft Exchange Server) for both public and private organizations.

Postbox

This program was created by one-time Mozilla employees and hence was based on Thunderbird. About ten years later, the software has developed into an autonomous and extremely effective mail client. The design of its interface is like that of other solutions, and it is also easy to use. Users who want a unique look can adjust themes or design their templates.

For a more efficient operation, Postbox makes use of different shortcuts. Users can access the Quick Bar via hotkey so that messages can be moved or categorized quickly. In addition, when creating an email, a signature can be entered with the use of the Quick Bar without having to use the mouse.

There are lots of benefits when writing emails in the postbox.

The software has various templates and text blocks that can be used to write cover letters and replies in a placeholder that can be added and created where the name of the receiver is always added automatically.

Thunderbird

For both private users and those in companies, Thunderbird is one of the most preferred options as an alternative to Outlook. The open-source solution is also available for free. The free version of the program is rather streamlined and offers only the most basic functions. One major advantage is the addition of various add-ons. This means that there is room for expansion for the email program. However, the add-ons and extensions are made to suit their respective versions. If there is a need to update your version of Thunderbird, the add-ons must be updated as well.

Spike

Spike was released in the year 2013 and it combines certain functions of classic email programs with those that are used in modern messenger apps.

Immediately a private mailbox is linked to the application, elements like subjects or signatures are no longer necessary, while the basic mail client functions, which include the central inbox or contact management, will be integrated into the modern messenger environment. It is also not coincidental that the creator of Spike described it as a conversational email application. Note that both audio and video calls can also be made via the software.

The spike depends on modern standards in terms of security. With just a single click, communications that also include attached files can be encrypted. This way, you can be sure your messages are fully protected against unwanted access. Spike is free for private users; however, monthly fees are charged when business email accounts are added.

Mailbird

Mailbird is an Outlook alternative that is only free in the test version. This email solution allows the unification of messages and contacts from different accounts into just one box. With different free themes, the interface can be designed as it best suits you.

Mailbird offers different interfaces to various applications and also enhances the mailbox with helpful features for better interaction and teamwork. For instance, Twitter, Whatsapp, Calendar, and Dropbox can be integrated into the mail to change it to a multi-functional program.

Outlook's Main Screen Using the Folder pane

The folder pane shows all the folders in Outlook. If this pane is minimized, other folders will not be displayed and you will not be able to gain access to them. There are two different ways this folder can be viewed.

The first is by;

Clicking on the left side of the screen. This will help in expanding the folder pane, making other folders visible.

The second option is to click on view, then the folder pane, click on normal so as to see things in a clearer way.

The folder pane in Outlook is said to be the main navigation tool between mailboxes, folders, and different modules like mail, calendar, and contacts. Note that the folder pane has a couple of different options and tips that can help make the pane fit more into your kind of style and help you work effectively and efficiently.

You can choose to enable or even disable the folder pane by Pressing the ALT + F1 buttons.

To change from one module to the other, make use of the icons enlisted in the lower area of the Folder pane. If you also prefer to see the names of the modules alone instead, disable the Compact Navigation through the Folder Pane Options dialog box.

Note that with the use of the Folder Pane, you can configure the way modules are shown and in the very order they are shown; they can also show module icons or names for easy navigation; add shortcuts to modules; and lots more.

To get the best out of this folder, you should spend some time clicking on various options, including the ones explained above.

The Information Viewer: Outlook's hotspot

The information viewer is the very place where most of the action in Outlook takes place. If we can assume the folder pane as being the channel sector on a TV, the information viewer will be more like the TV screen.

The information viewer is the very place where emails are read, contacts are searched for or added, and contact names are also displayed. If you also wish to do a whole lot of other fancy things like sorting contacts, tasks, and so on, the information viewer is the perfect place to get all of that and more done.

Based on the fact that lots of information, more than what can be seen at a glance, can be stored in Outlook, the information viewer helps to show a preview of the information available. This way, you are up to date with all you need to know. The calendar, for example, can store dates as far back as the 16's and as far ahead as you can imagine. The smallest calendar review that can be displayed is a day, and the largest calendar view is a month.

The information viewer also helps to arrange what it displays into smaller units known as "views." There is an option to create your own views and also save them, but you can also decide to use the view that comes with Outlook.

Move through the different previews of the information displayed by Outlook by clicking on various parts of the information viewer. Some people love to say they are browsing the information viewer when moving around it; it seems more like just scanning through the pages of a notebook.

You can also browse through the calendar data in the information viewer to keep you abreast of things to come.

To do that, simply follow the steps below:

Click on the calendar in the navigation bar or make use of the keyboard shortcut and press the Ctrl + 2 buttons.

 Next, click on the workweek button located on the Home tab of the ribbon. The workweek view of the calendar will then be displayed. Note that a workweek means 5 days if the regular calendar week shows 7 days.

To further spice things up, you can decide to change the appearance of the information viewer in several ways. For example, there might be a need to see the schedule for just a day or just the items that have been fixed for a particular category. Views can ensure that you get a glance at the very preview of information needed.

While checking out the calendar, you can also decide to check the To-Do bar located on the right side of the screen. The To-Do bar shows the appointments you have and also reminds you of things you need to do. To turn on this feature,

Click on the View tab located on the ribbon > click on the To-Do Bar > click the calendar button.

In Outlook, every module (mail, calendar, people, tasks, etc.) has its own version of the Ribbon, arranged specifically to meet the needs of the module. Most of all the buttons are visibly labeled with the very actions they are used for, such as replies, business cards, new appointments, and lots more.

A little button known as "properties" can be found in the lower-right corner of some groups.

Click on it if you want more information displayed than what is shown on the ribbon. Properties are also known as "dialog boxes" as they open some sort of dialog box launcher related to the group when it is clicked.

The Ribbon Ties Viewing Screen Tips

Each button located on the ribbon shows a little popup known as a "ScreenTip" when the mouse is placed over it. The ScreenTip informs you about the name of the button and also tells you things that will happen if you click on the button.

Some buttons have a small arrow that points downwards or to the right side of the button.

Click on the arrow to have a menu or list open. A very popular example, pertinent to almost all the modules in Outlook on the Home tab, is a button known as "Move." When you click on the Move button, it opens a menu and shows all the various places an Outlook item can be sent to.

Using the New Items Button

Each module in Outlook has a "New Items" button that enables the creation of an item in any module. For instance, if you are checking the name and address of a customer whose name was also mentioned in a very interesting article in one of the daily newspapers, you will want to remember to refer to it at any point in time. You can do this by creating a new item from the new contact option, selecting the particular date, and then saving it with the name of the customer or something unique that can always make you remember the incident in the daily diary.

Taking Peeks

One very unique feature in Outlook is a tiny pop-up window known as a "peek," which is displayed when you place your mouse over the modules such as People, Calendar, or Tasks in the navigation bar. This little but unique feature offers great help when giving a reply to an email about an event that needs to be scheduled. Feel free to take a quick peek at your calendar while you continue to work on that particular email. If a broader view with more information is needed, there is an option to make the peek window larger by clicking the button at the top right corner of the peek screen or by double-clicking on the calendar, people, or tasks in the navigation bar.

Getting Help in Outlook

The help feature in the Office applications, which includes Outlook, goes beyond just rendering help as it tries to get things done for you. Does that sound awkward? It isn't, it is just amazing and very helpful.

When working in the help feature, a lightbulb icon and a textbox are located at the top of the screen with the inscription, "Tell me what you want to do." Once that box is clicked, type in what you might need help with and it will display a list of things that starts with a list of things that can be done. For example, if you enter the word "delete," the help feature will bring up a link to the Delete and Delete All commands and also the folder with deleted items. When one of the commands is selected, it will delete the very Outlook item that has been chosen. When you click on "Deleted Items," it will take you straight to the deleted items folder.

Note that it is important that you request only the things that can be done in Outlook. If you type something like "what can I eat?", the choices Outlook will offer you might disappoint you. But if you are trying to do something that involves email, appointments, or tasks, Outlook should provide you with the very important links you need to get things done quickly.

Scroll beneath the list of links to view other choices that might be displayed by Outlook. Once you point at the "Get help" option, it will open a submenu of various help topics that are in some way related to what you have asked. You would have to click on that yourself, as there is no option to help you do that.

The final option in the help menu is called "Smart Lookup," which helps to open the Smart Lookup task pane and makes use of Microsoft Bing, which is the search engine for Microsoft, to search for the phrase that has been entered.

When using smart lookup, there may be a need to activate the intelligent service. For example, if you type "marry a millionaire" and click on the smart lookup link, a list of marriageable millionaires will be displayed, and if not, at least At the very least, you will get the definition of the word or phrase that has been typed and probably a link to Wikipedia also.

CHAPTER 5: EMAIL MASTERY 101

Email is very important for all professional communication in the office. If the organization you work with makes use of Outlook, learning how to make judicious use of it can be very vital to your professional development since the skills learned will help you arrange meetings with those you work with and also send email messages easily. Furthermore, you will be able to show your colleagues, boss, or team lead that you have learned well and improved over time when you make use of the features in Outlook with so much ease. You can even offer to teach them what they want you to know about the use of these tools.

Front Ends and Back Ends

There are basically two things needed to send and receive an email; a program that helps with the creation, saving, and management of messages and a program that actually sends the messages to people and also receives replies from them (exchanging messages). A few people in tech call these two parts the "front end" and "back end," as the case may be. Outlook, on the other hand, is a front end for email messages. It helps with the creation, formatting, storing, and management of messages, but it doesn't really do much about getting the message to the intended destination. Ensuring that messages get to their intended destination is the work of the back-end service (like the Microsoft Exchange Server in your office), the Internet Service Provider you use, and also by an online email service like outlook.com or gmail.com.

Email messages cannot be sent or received anywhere in the world without the use of an internet connection. The phone company you use most of the time provides internet services that can be used for this purpose. To ensure your email messages are sent quickly and you also get replies as quickly as possible, make sure you choose the best Internet Service Provider out there. Remember though, that the easiest choices aren't always the very best choices. There are several companies ready to offer internet services. Shop around to get the best value for money.

Creating Messages

In a lot of ways, electronic mail (email) is much better than the normal paper mail commonly known as snail mail. Email is delivered at a much faster pace (almost instantly) than paper mail. The speedy delivery can be of great help when closing a last-minute deal, sending across vital information towards the close of working hours, or for last-minute birthday greetings. Email is also very cheap to use; it is actually free most of the time.

The quick and dirty way

Creating a new email message can be very easy. Simply follow the steps below. Open Outlook The mail module will then be displayed, opening up the inbox.

Click on the New Email button Insert an email address in the To box. Insert a subject in the subject box.

Insert a message in the message box. And finally, click on the send button.

Most of the time, Outlook starts in the Inbox only. This will only change if the settings have been changed. If there is a need to start up in an entirely different folder than your inbox,

Click on the File tab and choose Options.

Click on the advanced option and in the Outlook Start and Exit part, change the Start Outlook. Click on the "browse" button to check all the folders in the Outlook data file. To begin in another module, select a folder that is similar to that module, e.g., Calendar or Notes.

The slow and complete way

You might like the more comprehensive way of creating an email message. If you love to create fancy emails, especially if you want to take advantage of every key feature Outlook has to offer, follow the steps below:

Locate the Mail module > select the New email button or press Ctrl + N. The new message form will then open up.

Click on the "To" text box and insert the email address of the person you are about to send a message to. If you are sending to more than one person, separate their email addresses with the use of either the comma or the semicolon. There is also an option of clicking on the To button itself, locating the names of the people you intend to send messages to in your address book, and double-clicking on their names to ensure they are added to the To text box.

Click on the Cc text box and insert the email address of the person whom you would like to have a copy of the email message you are about to send. You can also click on the "cc" button to include people from your address book.

Insert the subject of the message into the subject box. The subject should be very brief and simple, as it makes someone enthusiastic about reading your message rather than a very lengthy subject line. If for any reason, you forget to insert the subject, Outlook will open a window that asks if you really intend to send the message without a subject. Click on the "Don't Send" button to return to the message and include a subject. If there is really no need for a subject, click on the Send button to send the message.

Type the body of your message in the message box. If Microsoft Word is the word processor you use, you must be familiar with the graphics table, modes of formatting, and all the tricks in Word to ensure your email appears more attractive. These very same tricks can be found in Outlook by making use of the tools at the top of the message form on the Format Text tab.

Be extremely careful when formatting your email. This is because not all email systems can deal with graphics or text that has been formatted like boldface or italics. This way, the text you send to your client will not look like gibberish.

Furthermore, most people read their email on phones or phablets, which can make the text you send look odd. If you are not certain about how your recipient will receive your mail, stay off of adding graphics or formatting text.

Click on the Review tab > select the Spelling and Grammar button at the upper part of the message screen. You can also choose to press the F7 button.

Outlook will then run a spell-check to make sure your message is free of spelling and grammatical errors.

Finally, click on the send button or press Ctrl + Enter or Alt + S. Outlook will then move your email to the outbox. If you are connected to the internet, Outlook will send any message in the Outbox immediately. If the message was composed when you were not connected to the internet, click the F9 button to send the message again when you are connected to the internet. When a message has been sent, it will move to the sent folder automatically.

Another option for telling Outlook to send messages from the Outbox is to tap the little button looking like two envelopes overlapping that can be found on the Quick Access Toolbar at the top left corner of the Outlook window, which can be seen from any module in Outlook. If the mouse pointer is moved over this button, a screen tip will be displayed notifying that it is the send/receive all folders button. Whenever messages are sent by clicking on the send button in a message or by tapping the F9 button, it is also a way of telling Outlook to receive all messages coming in.

Setting priorities

Certain messages can be more important than others. Sending a report to your boss is not the same as sending a friendly message to a teammate or colleague. Setting the importance level of a particular message to "high" informs the recipient that the message needs urgent attention.

There are basically three levels of importance you can choose from:

- Low Normal High
- Setting sensitivity

There are times when there is a need for your message to be seen by only one person. Alternatively, you might just want to ensure your message is not altered by anyone after sending it. The sensitivity settings in Outlook help to put a restriction on what any other person might be able to do to your message after you have sent it. They also help you decide who that person can be.

In applying the sensitivity settings to a message.

Click to open the properties drop-down menu for messages.

Click on the list box arrow closest to the word "sensitivity" and any of the displayed levels as briefly described.

Most of the messages sent via Outlook have just the normal sensitivity, and this is what Outlook makes use of if the settings are not changed. Settings such as Private, Personal, and Confidential only inform those receiving the message that there might be a need to treat the message in a different way from the way they treat other normal messages. There are even certain organizations that employ the use of some strict measures in dealing with confidential messages.

Applying the sensitivity settings of a message to either private or confidential does not make it any different from other messages; all it does is inform the person receiving the message that the message has some information that might be delicate. If you use Outlook at work, make sure to double-check with your system administrators before assuming that the information you're about to send via email is secure.

Setting other message options

Upon clicking the Properties dialog box, you might see that there are quite a number of odd-sounding options. A few of these options are Request a Read Receipt for This Message (which informs you when the receiver reads the content of the message) and the Expires After option (this marks a message as expired if the receiver does not open the message before a stipulated time).

These options are quite useful. The only glitch is that your email and that of the email receiver must support the setting, else it might not work. If both of you are on the same network, making use of the Microsoft Exchange Server, all should work just fine. If you are both not using Outlook or an Exchange Network, it can just be a gamble.

Reading and Replying to Email Messages

Outlook has a number of methods to notify you when an email message has been received. The status bar located towards the left side of the Outlook screen will inform you of the total number of email messages you have in your inbox and the number of messages that are still unread. The word "inbox" will change automatically in the folder pane to a boldface form when there is an unread email. The titles of unread messages will also be bold.

To click open and read an email message, follow the steps below:

Locate the Mail Module: click on the title of the message you want to read twice. This will open up the message in its window.

Select the close tab option (X) or press the escape key to close the message pane when you are through.

Viewing previews of message text

At the time you begin to receive plenty of emails, some of them will be important, while others might not be very important, if not totally useless. Upon receiving the mail in your inbox, it can be very useful to know which is important and which is not. This way, you can focus on the very important one. You cannot depend on those sending the mail to tell you how important or otherwise it is. Outlook offers help by giving a glimpse at the first few lines of the message.

When launched, the message preview is always on and set to 1 line. This option can be changed to 2 or 3 lines, and you can also choose to turn it off totally. The Message Preview option becomes totally redundant if the reading pane is turned on, but if it is not, the preview can be a very useful feature.

To gain control over the previews of messages that have not been read, follow the steps below:

Find the Mail Module > click on the View tab option in the ribbon. Click on the Message Preview option.

Click on the setting you prefer (1 line, 2 lines, 3 lines, or off).

If, for any reason, there is a prompt to alter the settings found in all mailboxes or just this folder, select the option that works best for you.

All the modules in Outlook have a lot of viewing options that can be used to make information much easier to use. The Message Preview option is a very good way to scan through email if you don't want to make use of the reading pane.

Follow the steps below to set up the Reading Pane;

Locate the Mail Module >click on the View tab located on the Ribbon.

Select the Reading Pane option.

Select from the options on the right, bottom, or off.

Either of the options you decide to choose, you cannot be wrong. You can also switch from one choice to another if the first choice chosen is not comfortable for you.

Sending a reply

One of the amazing benefits of using email is that replying to a message is very easy. There is no need to know the person's address when replying; just click on the reply icon and Outlook will sort the remaining.

To reply to a message, follow the steps below:

Locate the Mail Module>select the title of the message that you want to reply to. If it is enabled, the selected message will be displayed in the reading pane.

Select one of the options below

To reply to those located in the From Field, select the Reply button.

To reply to those in the CC field and the From field, select the Reply All button. A reply screen will then open in the reading pane area where the initial message was before. Email sent to a bunch of people can also be received at once.

Ideally, it is expected that one person at the least will be named in the To field and more than one in the Cc field, which is for those you are sending just a copy of the email to. There is no need to keep replying to those in the CC field. You can also decide to reply to some of them if you wish.

Enter your reply into the message box. Do not be dismayed if you find out that the message box already has some messages in it; they are part of the message that you are replying to. The cursor blinking will be in the upper part of the screen. With this, anything you type will appear before the other message.

This means when you reply, the recipient can view the initial message to help refresh his or her memory about the discussion at hand.

Select the send button, and your message will be sent with the message form disappearing and the message replying to reappearing.

Press the escape key to close the message screen. This will make the message replied disappear and the inbox will reappear.

Resending messages

Asking people to do just what you want is another amazing feature of email. Nonetheless, most people overlook things because they receive too much email. When you discover you are making the same requests again, it is high time you took advantage of the resend feature in Outlook. With this, there will be no need to type the original request again; just find the original message and send it again with a lovely reminder about when the initial message was sent.

To send a message again, follow the steps below:

Locate the Mail Module and click on the sent items folder in the folder pane.

Search for the message with the initial request and click it twice. This will leave the original message unopened. Doing this is essential because resending a message is not done from the reading pane.

Select the Actions Button located on the Message Tab and then click on the Resend This Message option. This option will create a new copy of the former message automatically.

Insert a reminder or make certain changes to the message if need be.

Finally, click on the "Send" button.

Follow-up

Very often new mail will require certain tasks. Maybe your boss expects some contribution. One does not need to do that always instantly; it only needs to be done on time. I strongly recommend getting used to instantly telling Outlook when you'd like to get a reminder - in case you haven't done that in the meantime anyway. This way, it's much easier to get sorted and cluster your tasks instead of getting grinded between pressures from all sides. Outlook is your very reliable assistant and will make sure nothing will be left behind.

To get this done, in the open mail, in the Message tab, click Follow-up and for the whole choice of options, now on Custom….

The remainder will be set to due date and the end of office hours.

You should definitely adjust that to maybe the forenoon of that day when the first rush is done and you're still well before the closing date.

After clicking OK we can read in the email what settings were made.

Don't get caught by phishing

Some cunning people are always looking to trick and deceive you, and most of the time, it is always on the internet. Recently, a very common scam known as "phishing" has caused people to lose their time and money, causing them grief after responding to an email from an impostor who makes a claim to be a representative of a bank or certain financial institution.

If you receive an email claiming to be from a bank or any other business and you are asked to click on a link for verification of your personal data, don't do it.

Oftentimes, the link will take you to a website that seems genuine, but the data you are asked to enter can be used for theft or fraud. Reach out to the organization directly to be sure the email isn't fake. If you are unsure of what to do, it is best to delete such an email.

If, on the other hand, you actually want to check in with the sender of the email, visit your browser and check out the organization's website if it is one you are quite familiar with. If the message looks very old, please do stay away from it.

That's not my department: Forwarding Email

When you don't have the answers to an email you received, you may need to forward it to someone else who can.

Follow the steps below to forward a message;

Locate the Mail Module>select the title of the message you intend to send. The selected message will then be displayed in the reading pane.

Click on the Forward button. The forward screen will then be opened, replacing the reading pane. The subject of the initial message will also be the subject of the new message, with the exception of the letters FW, which means forward and is entered at the beginning.

Select the To text box and insert the email address of the person you intend to forward the message to. If the person is already in your address book, insert the person's name into the search box and Outlook will detect the email address.

Select the Cc textbox and insert the email address of those you want to send a copy of the message to. A lot of people forward very trivial things to their colleagues via mail. A host of recipients are always added as cc addresses.

Blind Copying for Privacy

Whenever a message is sent to a very large group, all those who get the message can view the email addresses in the To and Cc fields. This means email addresses that some might want to keep private have just been given out. Everyone might have received too many bizarre, unsolicited messages before, and most of them will get peeved at the broadcast of their messages without their permission.

Blind copies offer the best of both worlds. If all the email addresses were inserted into the Bcc field, no one's privacy would be compromised. By making use of Bcc addresses, addresses that need to be kept secret can be kept secret.

Deleting Messages

It is possible to disregard an email message without having to think twice. There might be no need to read it at all. By taking a glance at the inbox list, you already have an idea of the sender and the content of the message. Hence, there is no need to waste so much time reading some unnecessary jokes. Simply take it off.

If by accident, a message you still need is deleted, to undo the action very quickly, simply press the Ctrl + z button instantly. If some other actions have been committed in error, click on the

Deleted Items folder in the Folder pane; the messages that have been deleted in the past will be found there. To bring back a message that has been deleted, simply move it from the Deleted Items folder to the icon of whichever folder that it should be in.

To have a message deleted, follow the steps below:

Locate the Mail Module > select the title of the message that should be deleted. It is not a must to read the message. You can delete it from the list immediately.

Select the Delete button located on the Home tab on the Ribbon or simply click on the Delete key that is on the keyboard or press the Ctrl + D button.

The Delete button can be recognized easily; it is marked with a very big "X" sign, which simply means "Make this message disappear."

When messages are deleted, Outlook will not take off the deleted items; it simply drags them into the Deleted Items folder. (In some other mailing accounts and mail systems, it is known as trash rather than deleted items, though they mean the same thing.) If there are messages that have been unread in the Deleted Items folder, the name of the folder will be followed by the items that have not been read. It is possible to do away with the deleted messages forever by right- clicking on the Deleted Items folder located in the Folder pane and then selecting an empty folder. After the Deleted Items folder has been emptied, the messages in the folder will be gone forever.

Saving Interrupted Messages

If it happens that you get disturbed while composing an email, don't give up, as all is not lost. You can still get back to the mail. Whenever you begin to compose a message and then switch away to do other things without first sending the message, Outlook will save it automatically in the drafts folder.

To make sure it does this, Press the Ctrl + S keys before it saves automatically. When you are ready to continue working on the message being composed.

Click on the message and complete it by clicking on the send button.

You can also click on the "discard" button if you decide not to continue with the message.

Saving a Message as a File

There are times you receive an email that is so wonderful or disheartening and you want to have the email saved. You can decide to either print out the message or show it to someone else, save the message to a disk, or simply send the message to a desktop publishing program.

To save a message as a file, go through the following steps:

Locate the Mail Module with the message box open, choose the File tab on the Ribbon and then choose the Save As Option or select F12. This will open up the dialog box.

Make use of the navigation pane located on the left side of the save as box to select the drive and folder in which the file should be saved. Outlook will at first choose the document folder by default, but there is an option to save the message on any drive and folder as it suits you.

Select the File Name text box and insert the specific name you intend to give the file. Insert just any name you want. If you type a name that is not compatible with Outlook, it will bring up a window that states that the filename is not valid.

Select the triangle at the end of the save as type box and select text only as the file type. There are various file options to choose from, but the text-only file format is the one that is read the most by other applications.

The various file type options are:

Text Only: This file format is very simple and easy to use in that it helps to remove all of the message formatting. As the name implies, only text messages are saved.

This is a format that is used to save messages that will be frequently used in Outlook. It helps to save not just message formatting but also attachments.

Outlook Message Format: This format ensures all message formatting and attachments are kept but can be read by Outlook only.

This is just the same as the former file format, but it makes use of the international characters that can be read by any version of Outlook that makes use of various languages. This is Outlook's default setting.

This helps to save a message in a file format option that can be shown in a web browser like Edge or Firefox. Or any application that can show HTM or HTML files. File attachments are basically not saved, although the message formatting is always kept. Furthermore, in addition to saving a copy of the message with the HTM file extension, another different folder is created which has the supporting files that the HTM file needs.

This is also known as the HTML file format; the only exception is that an additional folder is not created due to the fact that all of the content is saved in just one file. Applications that can show HTM and HTML files should also be able to show MHT files.

Click on the save button and the message will be saved to the folder specified.

CHAPTER 6: ELEVATE YOUR EMAIL EXPERIENCE

Outlook has the capacity to perform lots of tricks with the email messages that are sent out and the ones that are received. Messages can be flagged with reminders, customized with signatures, or have special formatting added to the messages sent as replies.

Nagging by Flagging

Over the years, flags have become the most used feature in Outlook. If you are the type that receives hundreds of messages daily and needs help with remembering those you need to reply to so that they won't get lost in the mix, it is best to flag that message as soon as it is read. This way, you are sure you will get back to the sender. A flag can also be planted in a message that you send to others in order to remind them of a particular task they have to carry out for you and the person on the other end using Microsoft Outlook.

One-click flagging

If flagging a message serves as a reminder of what needs to be done in relation to a specific message, you should be aware of the quickest way to do so.

When you move your mouse over any message in the inbox, towards the very end on the right side, a gray outline flag will be displayed, looking more like a shadow flag. When that shadow is selected, the color will change from gray to red, which means it has been flagged. When you then check through your list of messages, you can easily recognize the one that needs more attention. This way, the tracklist of flagged messages can be maintained even if they are below the bottom of the screen.

Once you have sorted the messages you flagged, click on the flag again. This will replace the flag with a checkmark indicating that the message has been taken care of.

Setting flags for different days

If you select a message once to include a flag, a copy of the message will be displayed in the task list, and various tasks scheduled for that day will also be displayed. There are times when you might not be in the mood to deal with certain messages. You might feel it is better to wait till the next day or the next week. All you have to do is

Right-click on the flag and a list of possible dates for a flag will appear, including the next day, this week, next week, No date and customs will be displayed. Once a due date has been picked, it can still be changed if the need arises by moving the item from one due date to another with the use of the TO-DO bar. You can also choose to double-click on the item to have it reopened and then choose a different due date.

If the due date comes and goes and the flag remains unchanged, the message heading in the Inbox and To-Do bar will turn red.

Changing the default flag date

For those who are constantly busy or simply enjoy procrastinating, the default due date of flags can be changed by following the steps below;

Click on the "Follow Up" button located in the Tags group on the Ribbon. This will then have the flag shortcut displayed.

Select the Set Quick Click and a dialog box will be opened. The list in the box will provide different options for a due date.

Lastly, select the date that best suits you. The date will then become the default flag due date.

If you have issues committing yourself to a certain date, choose the "No Date" option and wait until someone raises an alarm.

Adding a flag with a customized reminder

Without a doubt, flags can actually do a whole lot more than just stand for a week or more. Flags in Outlook can pop up as a reminder, reminding you of what needs to be done. Flags can also be used to pester someone else when a reminder is attached to a message sent to someone else. Adding a reminder to a flag cannot be completed with a single click.

Follow the steps below to do that;

Locate the Mail Module and right-click on the message that needs to be flagged. The flag shortcut menu will then be displayed.

When this is done, the custom dialog box will then open up and if you click on the OK button at this point, the message will be flagged and ready for a reminder at 4 pm. This reminder can be adjusted, especially if the time is too close.

Select the list box arrow at the right side of the Flag to Text box and click on one of the menu items. A handy flag means "Follow Up" and reminds you to affirm a certain arrangement or appointment, as the case may be.

Insert the dates in the Start Date box, Due Date box, or all of the boxes. The date and time inserted will determine when a reminder will pop up to help jog the memory of the appointment. Ensure the dates are typed in a way Outlook will remember.

Click on the OK button. Once the reminder date that has been entered into the custom dialog box is up, the reminder dialog box will then help to offer a nudge.

Changing the date on a reminder

Don't get nagged with a reminder; you can always pull it off and do it much later.

To change the date on a reminder that was sent to you by someone else, follow the following steps:

Locate the Mail Module and select the message that has the reminder that needs to be changed. The message will be displayed as highlighted when it has been selected. To open the custom dialog box, simply right-click on the message.

Click on the Home tab and select the Follow Up on the Ribbon option, then include a reminder. As an alternative, press the Ctrl+Shift+G buttons.

Click on the Reminder checkbox and, if it has not yet been selected, choose a new date for the reminder flag to show up. If the checkbox has already been selected, leave it as if you click on it again, it will then leave it deselected.

Finally, click on the OK button.

There is also an option to click on the snooze button in the reminder dialog box to turn off the reminder flag for some time when it pops up, the same way it is done with the alarm clock.

Saving Copies of Your Messages

There is nothing handier than having to know what has been sent and when exactly it was sent. All outgoing email messages in Outlook can be saved. This way, you can always go back and check the message that has been sent.

Immediately after the Outlook program is installed on a computer, it starts saving sent messages. This feature can, however, be turned off. Before attempting to do so, check your message folder to be sure it contains sent messages.

To save copies of the messages, simply follow the steps below.

Choose the File tab > select the Options button. This will then open up the Outlook dialog box.

Select the Mail button and locate the navigation window on the left side. The mail settings will then be displayed.

Move down to the Save Messages section and click on the Save copies of the messages in the Sent Items folder check box if it hasn't already been selected.

Then finally click on the OK button.

Setting Your Reply and Forward Options

The look of a forwarded message can be controlled as well as the replies. If you use Microsoft Outlook, your text can be made to look really incredible in your messages by the addition of graphics, special effects, or some wild-looking fonts. If mail is being sent to people who use other programs and not Microsoft Outlook or to those using web-based email services like Gmail, some of the effects might not be well translated.

To set your options, follow the steps below:

Click on the File tab, locate the ribbon, and click on the Options icon. The options dialog box for Outlook will then open up.

Select the Mail button located in the navigation window on the left side and the mail settings window will then be opened.

Move downwards to the Replies and Forwards section and select the list box arrow at the right side of the Reply to a Message box. A menu of options will then be displayed, including the original text as the default option. The diagram located on the left side of the menu will show how the message will be displayed when each option is chosen.

Select the preferred style to use for replying to messages. A little diagram on the left side of the menu will change instantly to display what your choice will look like. You can try another if you don't like the choice you made earlier.

Click on the list box arrow that can be seen on the right side of the When Forwarding a Message box. This menu option looks almost the same as the one above, with just one fewer choice.

Select the style preferred to be used for forwarding messages.

Click on the OK button. The Outlook Options dialog box will then be opened.

By making use of Outlook, there is so much room to explore and do all sorts of fancy and even useful tricks with email. If the advanced options menu appears confusing, you can easily ignore them and just click on the Reply button and insert your reply.

You can also choose to delete the original message when a forward is created or replied to, but it's best to include at least a part of the original message. This way, it will make the response easier to understand. There is also an option to choose and delete some parts of the main text that are not relevant to your reply.

Sending Attachments

If you have created a document in another application and you don't want to send it just yet, there is no need to type the same message all over again in Outlook; simply send the document as an attachment to an email message. Word processing documents, spreadsheets, and other presentations such as PowerPoint can all be attached. You can also choose to include pictures and music; any type of file can be sent as an attachment.

The Send From menu is the simplest way to send a file from a Microsoft Office program such as Microsoft Word.

Open up the file in the program it has been created in. Choose the File tab option located on the ribbon.

Select the "share" button.

Choose the Word document from the share dialog box and write the message in Outlook.

If you don't want that option, you can have a message sent directly from Outlook by following the steps below.

Locate the Mail Module and select the New Email button that can be found on the Ribbon. You can also press the Ctrl + N button if you prefer to use a shortcut.

Choose the Attach File button found on the New Message form's Ribbon.

A list will then drop down to display the names of the files that have recently been worked upon.

You may be lucky enough to find the name of the file there, then just click on it. If the name of the file is not there, select the Browse This PC option located at the lower part of the screen. This will then open up the Insert File Dialog Box.

Click on the name of the preferred file and tap the send button. The name of the file will then be displayed in the Attached box in the message form's message header. When the email message is sent, a copy of the selected file will be sent to the recipient.

Enter a message if you have one to send. There might be no message and you just want to send an attachment. Take note that the content of the attachment will not be displayed on the screen of the recipient until the attachment is opened.

Click on the "To" button in the message form. The dialog box for choosing names will then be displayed.

Choose a name from the contact list and click on the button in the Select Names dialog box. This will then open up the name of the person that has been selected. This process can be repeated if you want to include more than one recipient.

Select the OK button. The name of the person can now be found in the To box of the message.

Click on the Subject text box and insert a subject for the message. The option of a subject is not compulsory, but if you want the message to look important, a subject can be helpful.

Finally, click on the "send" button.

Emailing Screenshots

It is often said that pictures are worth more than a thousand words. Most of those words become four-letter words when the computer begins to act up. This makes it very difficult to describe the type of problem in an accurate manner.

When problems like this arise, Outlook can be of help.

A screenshot is simply a picture of the screen of a computer that is captured to show what is being done on the computer at that point in time. This book contains lots of screenshots to make certain steps and procedures more comprehensible. The exact same thing can be done with the screenshot feature in Outlook. A screenshot can be sent to help a person solve a problem with his or her computer. A screenshot can be sent off just about anything, including pictures and documents. The possibilities of this feature are endless.

To include a screenshot in an email message, simply follow the steps below.

When an email message or a reply is being composed, select the Insert tab on the ribbon. If you notice the screenshot button is grayed out, ensure the cursor is inside the body of the email message.

Tap the screenshot button. This will then display a gallery of thumbnail images.

Choose any one of the screens from the gallery. The screenshot that has been chosen will then be displayed in the body of the email message.

Conclude with your email message and send it to the recipient.

Creating Signatures for Your Messages

Most people love to include signatures at the very end of the messages they send. A signature, most of the time, is just a few lines of text that show you to all those that read your message and also states certain things you want them to know. Lots of people include their names, the names of their businesses, and also the web addresses, their motto, and a little personal information. You can set Outlook to automatically include a signature in all outgoing messages, but a signature file must be created first. To create a signature Choose the File tab found on the Ribbon > Click on the Options button. This will then open the Outlook Options dialog box.

Select the Mail button in the navigation window towards the left side. This will open up the Mail settings window.

In the Compose Message section, click on the signature button. The signature and stationery dialog box will then be open.

Click on the New Button icon.

The dialog box for a new signature will open.

Enter a name for the new signature. The name that is typed will then be displayed in the New Signature box.

Click on the OK button to complete this process. The dialog box for the new signature will then close.

Enter the text of the type of signature that you prefer in the Edit Signature box and include any formatting that suits you. To apply changes to font, color, size, or other text characteristics, make use of the button in the text box. You can choose to make the signature in Word and then copy and paste it in the Edit Signature box.

Shortcuts worth taking

The following tips will help you boost your productivity, including turning a message into a meeting and resending it. You can boost your Outlook productivity with these ten accessories, including Skype, OneDrive, and an online service for backing up your data.

Also learn why you cannot have a unified inbox in Outlook as well as how you cannot create a distribution list from an email.

Using the New Items Tool

In whatever module you are in, click the tool on the far-left side of the ribbon to add a new item.

So you change the name and appearance of this icon when you change modules, so it becomes the New Task icon when you switch to the Task module, the New Contact icon when you switch to the People module, and so forth.

Alternatively, you can click the New Items tool just to the right of it to access the menu.

New Items allows you to create a new item in a module other than the one you're in without switching modules.

You might want to create a task while you're answering an email. Choose Task from the list of new items, create your task, then continue working with your email.

Sending a File to an Email Recipient

Using Outlook email, you can send a file with just a few mouse clicks, regardless of whether Outlook is running.

If you're using File Explorer to view your files, you can mark any file for sending to any recipient.Here's what you need to do:

Use File Explorer to locate the file. To send a file, right-click on it.

You are presented with a menu.

Choose the recipient. A new menu appears.

Select the recipient of the mail. There is a form for new messages.

The attached file is represented by an icon in the attached box.

Include the subject of the file and the email address of the person you're sending it to.

Adding a comment to your message is as simple as typing it in the message area.

Click the "Send" button.

The message is delivered to the receiver.

The Outbox receives your message.

Turning a Message Into a Meeting

Occasionally, after exchanging dozens of email messages about a topic, it would be faster to talk. Creating a meeting from an email message is as easy as clicking the Meeting button on the Home tab (in the Inbox with the appropriate

You can then create a meeting based on the contents of the email by clicking on the New Meeting button.

Finding Something

You can accumulate a lot of items in Outlook in no time, which can then take a while to search through when you are looking for one specific item.

Outlook can help you find items quickly if you type the name of the item in the search field at the top. That launches a quick search, so you can find what you are looking for in no time.

Undoing Your Mistakes

It's time you learned about the Undo command if you didn't already. The Ctrl + Z shortcut key can be used to undo accidentally entered text, as can the Undo button in the upper left corner of the screen in the Quick Access Toolbar.

You can experiment without worrying about the consequences; the worst thing you can do is undo it!

Using the "Go to Date" Dialog Box

Any calendar view can be accessed using the "Go to Date" dialog box. You'll find it under the "Go-To" group on the Home tab, under Properties. You can also use Ctrl + G as a shortcut.

Adding Items to List Views

You can add an item to a list at the top of most Outlook lists by typing something into the blank field. Simply click the "Add a New Task" button to begin.

Your new item will be entered into the field once you click on it.

Sending Repeat Messages

Since you might send out one or two messages repeatedly,

store them as Quick Parts to save time.

The steps you should follow when finding an Outlook accessory vendor online are:

Your email message should be addressed.

The email address of the company appears in my browser.

Select the Insert tab.

Click the Quick Parts button in the message body.

Your saved AutoText item will appear.

Make certain changes to reflect the name of the product.

Click on the "Send" button.

Your request can be sent in less than 30 seconds, and you can then move on to the next task.

Using this feature requires you to first store text blocks in Quick Parts:

Choose the text you want to repeat in an email message, appointment, contact record, meeting, or task.

Select the Insert tab.

To access Quick Parts, click the Text group button.

Select "Save Selection to Quick Part Gallery."

You can organize Quick Part text into groups according to their purpose. You could, for instance, generate the text for introductory messages and closing messages for different types of messages and then store them.

Resending a Message

When someone forgets to do something, you asked them to do, sometimes you need to remind them.

A new message could be written, saying to that person how often you've reminded him or her already.

However, this is quicker and easier:

Open your Sent Items folder.

Go back to the message you sent last time and click it twice. Decide what action to take.

You can resend this message by choosing this option.

Additionally, you could add the following: "Here is another copy in case you didn't receive the first."

CHAPTER 7: KEYBOARD SHORTCUTS IN OUTLOOK

Frequently used shortcuts

To do this	Press
Create a new message or calendar event.	Ctrl+N
Open selected message in a new window.	Shift+Enter
Delete message or item.	Delete
Forward message.	Ctrl+F
Go to calendar.	Ctrl+2
Select the **Reply All** option.	Ctrl+Shift+R
Reply to email message.	Ctrl+R
Send email message.	Ctrl+Enter
Open split buttons.	Alt+Down arrow key

Edit text

To do this	Press
Copy your selection to the clipboard.	Ctrl+C
Cut text you selected.	Ctrl+X
Delete selected text or characters to the left of the cursor.	Backspace

To do this	Press
Delete the word to the left of the cursor, but not the space before the word.	Ctrl+Backspace
Insert a hyperlink.	Ctrl+K
Paste content from the clipboard into the current location.	Ctrl+V
Repeat the most recent action.	Ctrl+Y
Reverse the most recent action.	Ctrl+Z

Format text

To do this	Press
Apply bold formatting.	Ctrl+B
Apply italic formatting.	Ctrl+I
Underline text.	Ctrl+U

Mail keyboard shortcuts

To do this	Press
Collapse the selected section.	Left arrow key
Expand the selected section.	Right arrow key

Use the message and reading list

To do this	Press
Delete selected message.	Delete

To do this	Press
Mark the selected conversation or message as read.	Ctrl+Q
Mark the selected conversation or message as unread.	Ctrl+U
Permanently delete the selected message or item.	Shift+Delete
Flag a message or mark a flagged message as complete.	Insert
Cancel a search.	Esc
Go to the next message	Ctrl+>
Go to the previous message	Ctrl+<

Use the message list

To do this	Press
Select the current and next message in the list. Use this to select multiple, contiguous messages.	Shift+Down arrow key
Select the current and previous messages in the list. Use this to select multiple, contiguous messages.	Shift+Up arrow key
Select the first message in the folder.	Home or Ctrl+Home

Use the reading list

To do this	Press
Close a new message.	Esc
Create a new message.	Ctrl+N
Forward a selected message.	Ctrl+F
Go to the bottom of a conversation or message.	End
Go to the top of a conversation or message.	Home
Move down one page for conversations or messages of two or more pages.	Page down
Move up one page for conversations or messages of two or more pages.	Page up
Reply to the selected message.	Ctrl+R
Reply to the sender and all recipients of the selected message.	Ctrl+Shift+R
Send a message.	Ctrl+Enter

Calendar keyboard shortcuts

To do this	Press
Create a new calendar item.	Ctrl+N
Delete the selected item.	Delete
Go to the calendar.	Ctrl+2
Move to a different region in the calendar.	F6

To do this	Press
Move to the next event or area in the current view.	Tab key
Move to a previous event or area in the current view.	Shift+Tab
Open the selected item.	Enter

Use the calendar board view

To do this	Press
Open the Quick Switcher.	Ctrl+Shift+K
Pan left, right, up, or down.	Ctrl+Left, Right, Up, or Down arrow key With JAWS and NVDA, switch to focus navigation to use this shortcut.
Reset pan and zoom.	Ctrl+0
Move selected item left, right, up, or down.	Ctrl+Shift+Left, Right, Up, or Down arrow key With JAWS and NVDA, switch to focus navigation to use this shortcut.
Deselect all items.	Esc
Open **Board** view.	Shift+Alt+6

Contacts (People) keyboard shortcuts

To do this	Press
Go to **People**.	Ctrl+3
Go to **Mail**.	Ctrl+1
Go to **Calendar**.	Ctrl+2
Delete a contact or contact list.	Delete or Ctrl+D
Create a contact.	Ctrl+N
Search for a contact.	Ctrl+E
Discard contact.	Esc
Save a contact or contact list.	Ctrl+S
Select all contacts or contact lists.	Ctrl+A
Unselect all contacts or contact lists.	Esc
Edit a contact or contact list.	Shift+E
Move down in the contact list or hub list.	Down arrow key
Move up in the contact list or hub list.	Up arrow key
Create a contact list.	Ctrl+L
Display the list of **People** keyboard shortcuts.	Shift+Question mark (?)
Move the focus to the **Home** tab.	Alt+Windows +H
Move the focus to the **View** tab.	Alt+Windows +V

CONCLUSION

Embracing the Digital Transformation with Outlook 2024

As we reach the conclusion of the "Microsoft Outlook Quick Start 2024 Guide," it's important to reflect on the journey we've embarked upon. This guide has not just been about learning a software application; it has been about embracing the digital transformation that is reshaping our world. Microsoft Outlook 2024, with its myriad of features and functionalities, stands at the forefront of this transformation, offering tools and capabilities that extend far beyond traditional email management.

The Journey Through Outlook 2024

Throughout this guide, you've been introduced to the comprehensive and multifaceted nature of Outlook 2024. From setting up your account to mastering advanced features for email, calendar, and task management, each chapter has been a step forward in your journey to becoming an Outlook expert. You've learned to navigate the interface, customize settings, manage emails efficiently, schedule and organize tasks and meetings, and much more.

Customization and Personalization: A Key Theme

A recurring theme in this guide has been the power of customization and personalization. Outlook 2024, with its flexible interface and customizable features, allows you to tailor the application to fit your unique needs and preferences. Whether it's through creating rules for email management, customizing the calendar view, or setting up tasks and reminders, Outlook 2024 can be molded to become your personalized tool for productivity and communication.

Security and Privacy in Outlook 2024

In the digital age, the importance of security and privacy cannot be overstated. Throughout this guide, we've emphasized Outlook 2024's robust security features, from spam filters and phishing protection to encryption options for sensitive information. Understanding and utilizing these features is crucial in safeguarding your digital communications and personal data.

Collaboration and Connectivity

Another significant aspect of Outlook 2024 is its facilitation of collaboration and connectivity. We've explored how Outlook serves as a central hub for teamwork, allowing for shared calendars, group task management, and efficient scheduling of meetings. In a world where remote work and digital collaboration are becoming increasingly prevalent, these features are invaluable in maintaining connectivity and productivity.

The Evolution of Email Management

Email management has been a central focus of this guide. Outlook 2024's advanced features, such as focused inbox, categorization, and powerful search functionalities, transform how we handle email communication. These tools enable you to manage large volumes of emails effectively, ensuring that your inbox aids rather than hinders your productivity.

Outlook as a Reflection of Changing Digital Communication Trends

As you've journeyed through this guide, you've witnessed how Outlook 2024 reflects the changing trends in digital communication. It's not just about sending and receiving emails; it's about managing your digital life in an integrated, efficient, and productive manner. The skills and knowledge you've gained here are not just about using a software application; they're about adapting to and thriving in the digital world.

Looking Forward

As we conclude this guide, it's important to recognize that the world of digital communication and productivity tools is ever-evolving. The skills and knowledge you've acquired from the "Microsoft Outlook Quick Start 2024 Guide" provide a strong foundation, but the journey doesn't end here. Continuous learning and adaptation are key in staying adept in an ever-changing digital landscape.

The Power of Integration

A key aspect of Outlook 2024 is its ability to integrate seamlessly with other tools and services. This guide has shown you how Outlook can work in harmony with various applications, enhancing not just email management but also your overall productivity and workflow efficiency. The integration capabilities mean that Outlook is not just a standalone application but a central hub in your digital ecosystem. Whether it's syncing with your phone's contacts or integrating with cloud storage services, Outlook 2024 makes it all possible in a cohesive and user-friendly manner.

Navigating Through the Outlook Ecosystem

Throughout this guide, we have navigated the comprehensive ecosystem of Outlook 2024, exploring its many facets and functionalities. You've learned how to leverage its robust calendaring system, manage tasks effectively, and utilize contacts for more than just email addresses. These features, when used to their full potential, turn Outlook into a powerhouse of organization, keeping you on track with your personal and professional objectives.

Outlook 2024: A Tool for All

One of the most compelling aspects of Outlook 2024, as highlighted in this guide, is its versatility. Whether you're a business professional managing a hectic schedule, a student coordinating academic deadlines, or someone trying to keep up with personal commitments, Outlook 2024 is designed to cater to a wide range of needs and lifestyles. This adaptability makes it an invaluable tool for users from all walks of life.

Mastering Efficient Communication

Efficient communication is at the heart of Outlook 2024, and this guide has equipped you with the skills to master this art. From crafting impactful emails to managing group communications, Outlook offers a suite of features to enhance your communication skills. The guide has emphasized not just the technical aspects of these features but also the best practices and etiquette of digital communication, ensuring that you convey your messages effectively and professionally.

Embracing Future Trends and Updates

As technology continues to advance, Outlook will undoubtedly evolve to incorporate new trends and features. This guide has provided a foundation, but it's important to stay abreast of future updates and enhancements. Embracing these changes and continuously learning will ensure that you remain proficient in using Outlook, regardless of how the digital landscape evolves.

The Impact of Outlook 2024 on Personal Productivity

The impact of Outlook 2024 on personal productivity cannot be overstated. As you apply the learnings from this guide, you'll notice a significant improvement in how you manage time, tasks, and communications. The ability to organize and prioritize with Outlook's tools can lead to a more structured and less stressful daily routine, ultimately contributing to a better work-life balance.

The Role of Outlook in the Broader Digital World

Outlook 2024 is more than just an email client; it's a reflection of the broader digital world we live in. This guide has shown how Outlook can be a gateway to understanding broader digital trends, from remote work and digital collaboration to data security and privacy. By mastering Outlook, you're not just improving your efficiency with one tool; you're enhancing your ability to navigate the digital world confidently.

Concluding Thoughts

As this guide comes to a close, it's important to reflect on the journey you've undertaken. The "Microsoft Outlook Quick Start 2024 Guide" has been a comprehensive exploration of Outlook 2024, but it's also been a guide to understanding and adapting to the digital communication landscape. With the skills and knowledge you've gained, Outlook 2024 will be a vital tool in your arsenal, helping you to communicate effectively, organize efficiently, and ultimately, achieve your personal and professional goals in an increasingly digital world.

Final Thoughts

Thank you for joining us on this comprehensive journey through Microsoft Outlook 2024. Whether you use Outlook for personal organization, professional communication, or collaborative projects, the insights from this guide will help you navigate and leverage Outlook's capabilities to their fullest. As you continue to use Outlook 2024, remember that it is more than just a tool; it's a partner in your journey towards greater productivity and effective digital communication.

Here's to mastering Outlook 2024 and beyond, as you continue to navigate the exciting and dynamic world of digital communication and organization.

Printed in Great Britain
by Amazon

43875914R00056